A Penny to a Dollar by QL Walker

Illustrated by Zeeshan Shahid
Published by QuWalk LLC

In Honor of
Mom and Dad

To Nay and Zel, I love you with all my heart.

To My siblings, I adore you.

A special thank you to Aunt Valerie, Jules, Debra, Talisha, Shondelle, ZaQia and Shevan
for their invaluable support and feedback.

Proverbs 13:11 NIV
Dishonest money dwindles away, but whoever gathers money little
by little makes it grow.

On the second floor of a building in Harlem lives the Coin family, consisting of Daddy Dollar, Mommy Hess, Penelope, and Tyme.

Life at home is simple; the Coin family turns everyday activities into a learning experience.

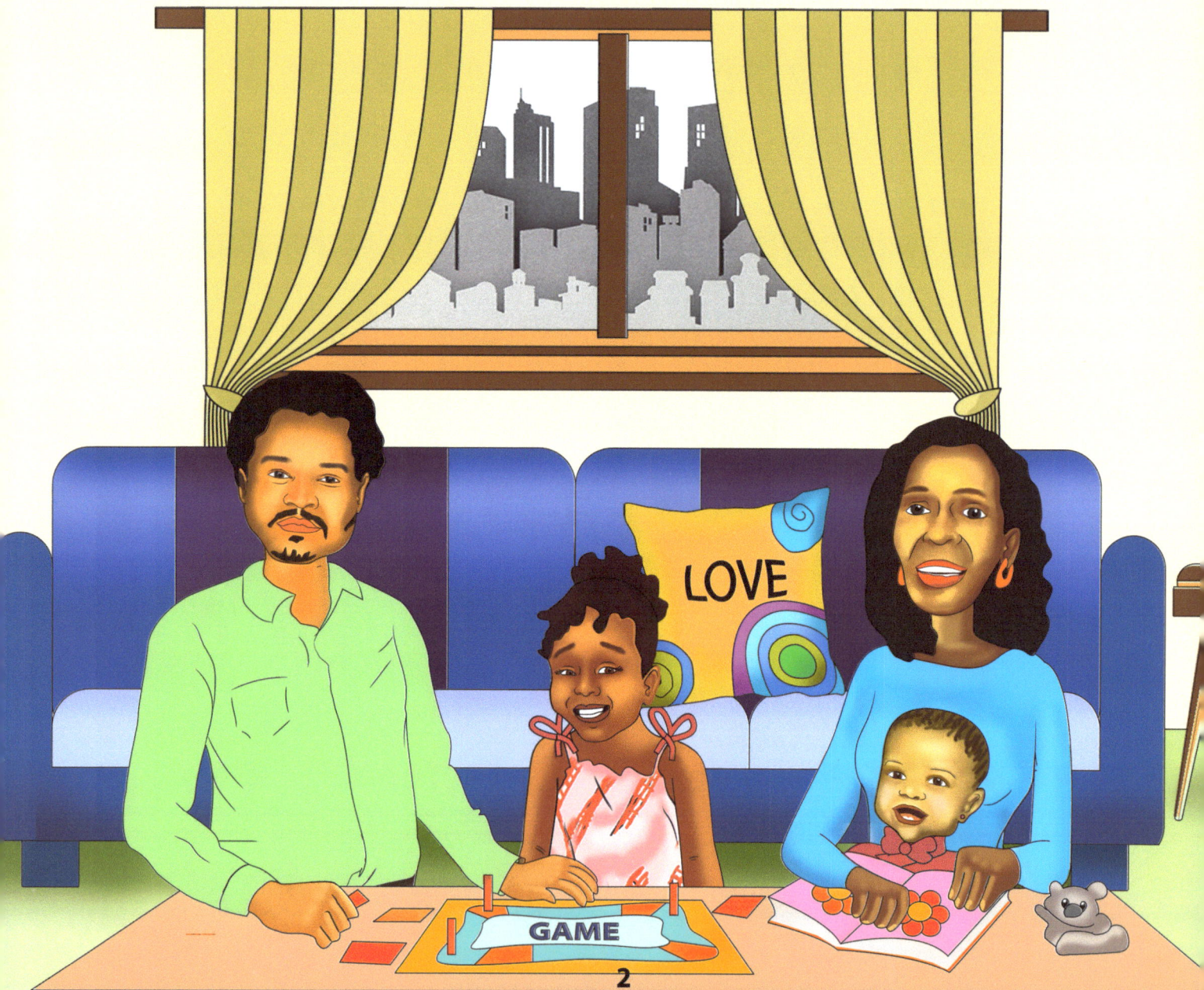

2

Daddy Dollar is open, honest, and can fix anything! He works hard and always puts family first.

Daddy Dollar got his nickname because he always talks dollars and sense.

4

Not a day goes by that Daddy Dollar does not check prices and remind you how much an item cost when he was your age.

You often hear Daddy Dollar saying, "Money does not grow on trees; money comes from working hard and working smart."

WORK HARD
WORK SMART

"Money doesn't grow on trees"

Daddy Dollar adores his children but believes that children should be loved not spoiled. He has special names for Penelope and Tyme. He calls Penelope **"Pee Wee"** because she is the firstborn, and he calls Tyme **"Facey"** because she makes funny faces.

Mommy Hess works in the home; her hobby is collecting loose change and looking for ways the family can save and earn extra money.

Mommy Hess does not believe in being wasteful; she donates gently-used items to charity. She loves redesigning old furniture and using it again.

She is funny, yet stern and enjoys making people laugh.

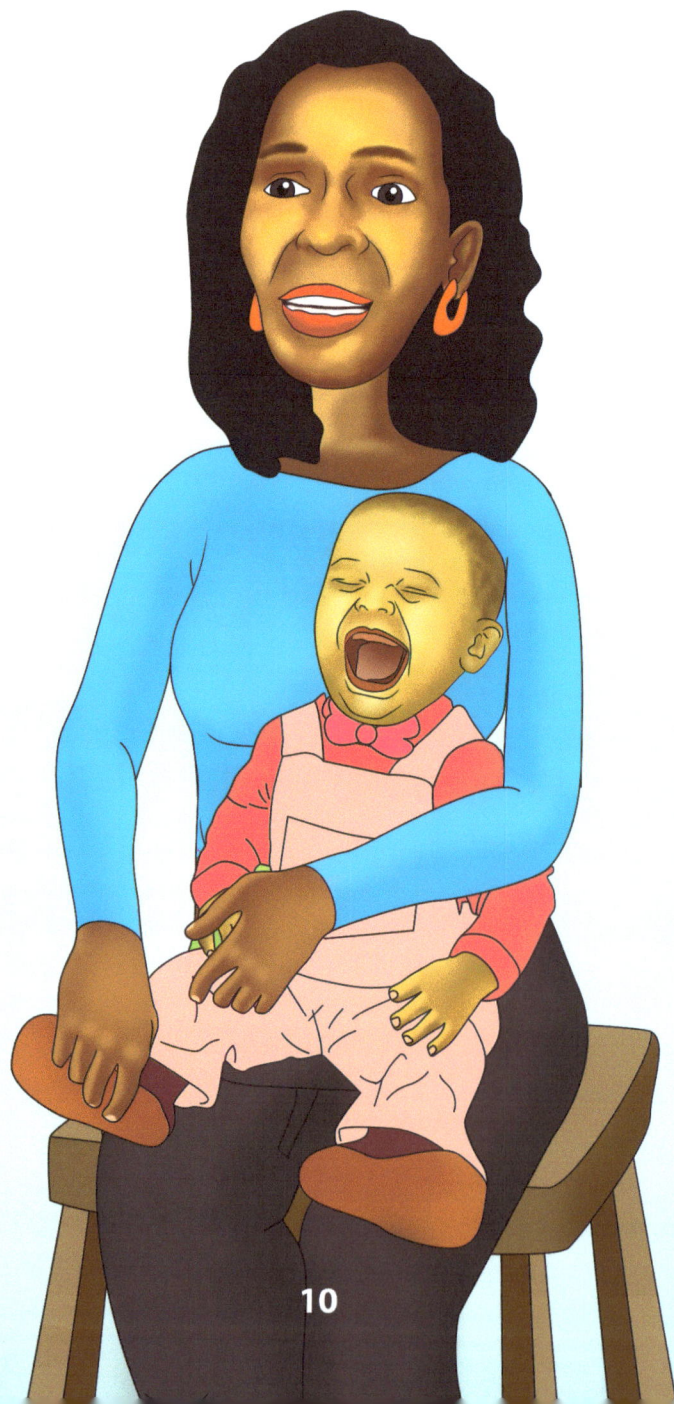

Penelope loves the color pink, she is very curious, and she is always asking lots and lots of questions.

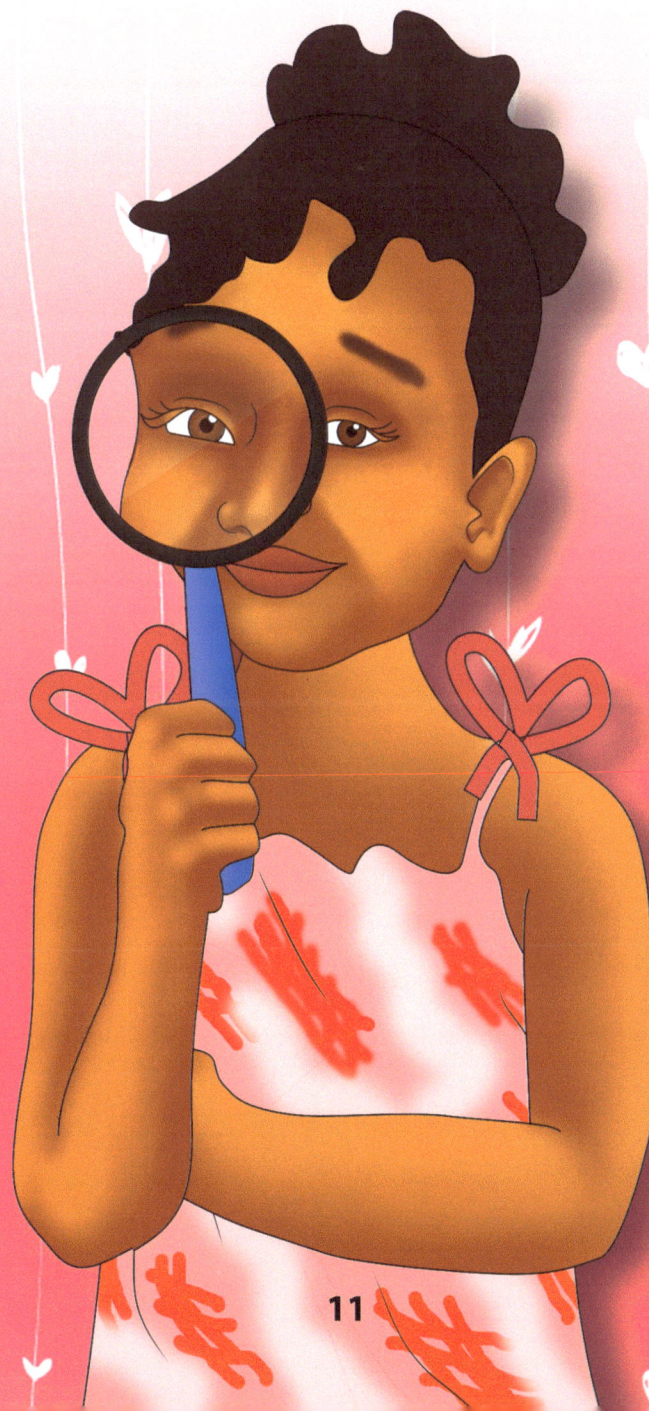

Being the firstborn, a lot is wished upon Penelope. Daddy Dollar and Mommy Hess want her to get good grades, behave well, practice her manners, and set a good example for her younger sister.

Sheila, Mommy Hess's oldest sister, and her daughter Crystal live upstairs. Penelope looks up to her cousin Crystal. She smiles with excitement when she sees her as she usually gives Penelope a crisp dollar bill. Penelope tucks the dollar away and later puts it in her piggy bank.

13

Penelope will be starting preschool, and Daddy Dollar believes that children should learn at home first. He says that adults should **"Start early and talk to them often."** **"Parents are the first teachers"** is his philosophy.

$$\$\$ \quad \text{Vote} \quad \text{STEM} \quad \text{Dollar} \quad \text{Motivation}$$

Management $\$\$ Vote STEM Savings Dollar Motivation
Future Retirement
Success Team VISION
Keep your Invest
WORD Coins Add up

Daddy Dollar loves numbers, and saving is the family's passion. Since Penelope will be starting school, they thought it would be fitting to give Penelope a lesson on money.

The Coin Family
Spending Plan
Serve
Save
Spend

Daddy Dollar says to Mommy Hess, "Take these coins and place them around the house, and tell Penelope that all the coins she finds she can keep!"

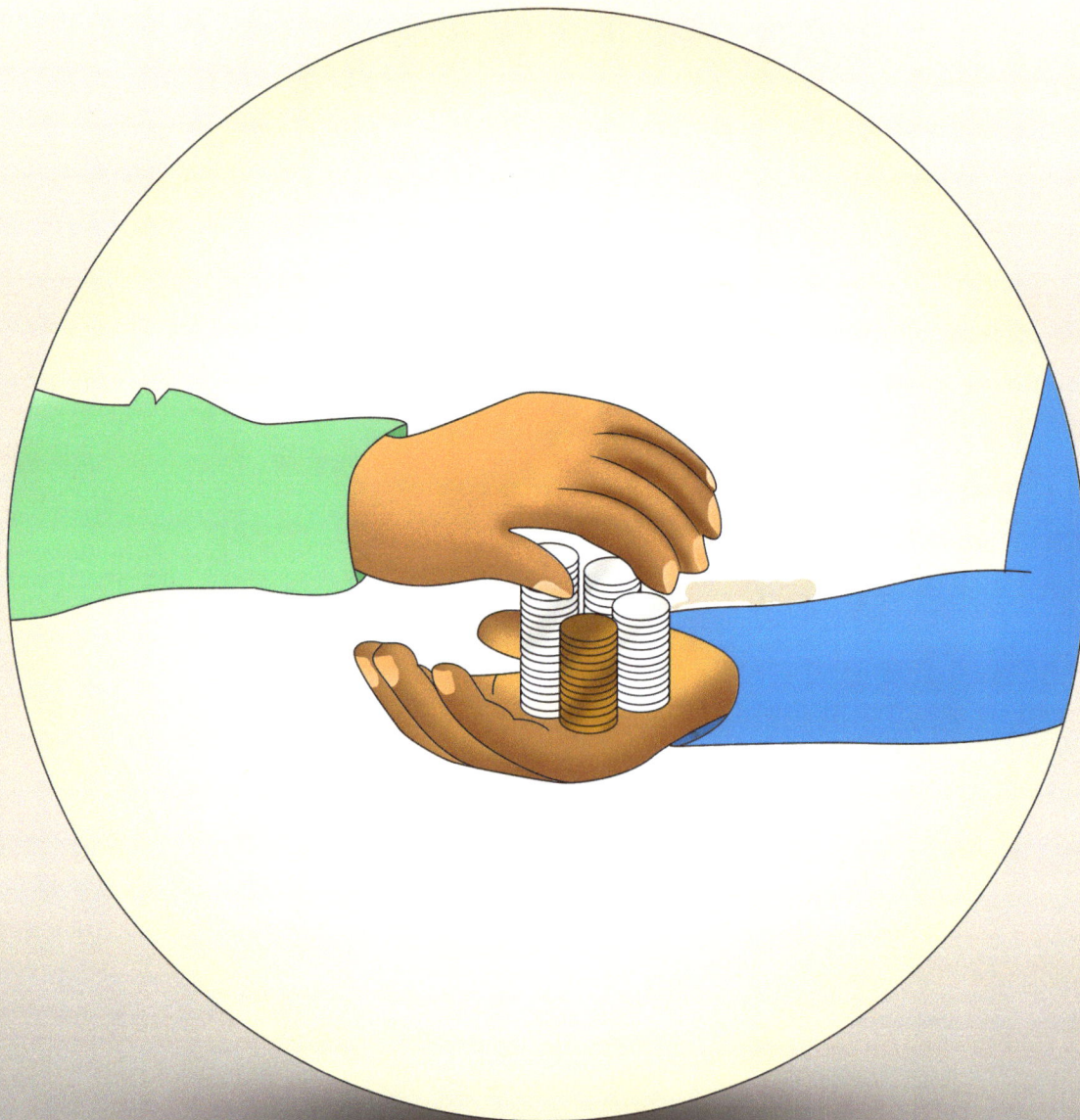

Mommy Hess takes five pennies, five nickels, two dimes, and two quarters and places them around the house.

Penelope first sees the pennies, looks at them and says,
"Daddy Dollar, I want money that folds."

Coins are valuable. They are useful and important in our everyday lives. Daddy Dollars says "Pee Wee, without a penny, you will never have a dollar."

"Have a seat and place your hands on the table; it's time for a lesson on coin values." says Daddy Dollar. " Pee Wee, one finger, one penny. One penny equals one cent."

One Penny = One Cent

"Two fingers, two pennies. Two pennies equal two cents.
Three fingers, three pennies. Three pennies equal three cents.
Four fingers, four pennies. Four pennies equal four cents," says Daddy Dollar.

Two Pennies = Two Cents

Three Pennies = Three Cents

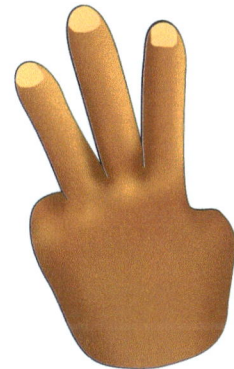

Four Pennies = Four Cents

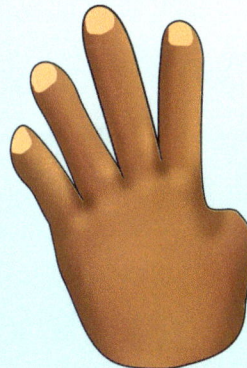

"Five fingers, five pennies." Daddy Dollar says,
"Pee Wee, five pennies equal a nickel."

Five Pennies = A Nickel

Daddy Dollar pulls another nickel out of the bank; he says, "To get 10 cents,
you need two nickels or 10 pennies. Two nickels equal 10 cents,
or 10 pennies equal 10 cents. "

Two Nickels = A Dime

Ten Pennies = A Dime

"To get a quarter, 25 cents, you need 25 pennies, or 5 nickels, or two dimes and a nickel. "

5 nickels

25 Pennies

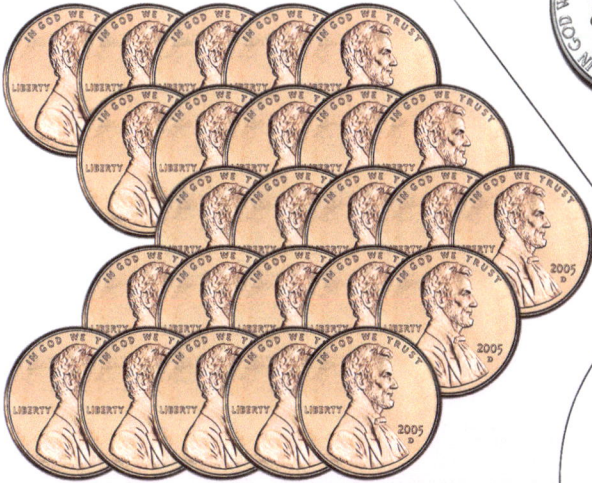

2 Dimes 1 Nickel

1 Quarter

"Four quarters equal a dollar, 10 dimes, 20 nickels, or 100 pennies."
Daddy Dollar pulls a crisp dollar bill out of his wallet to show
how the coins add up to a paper dollar.

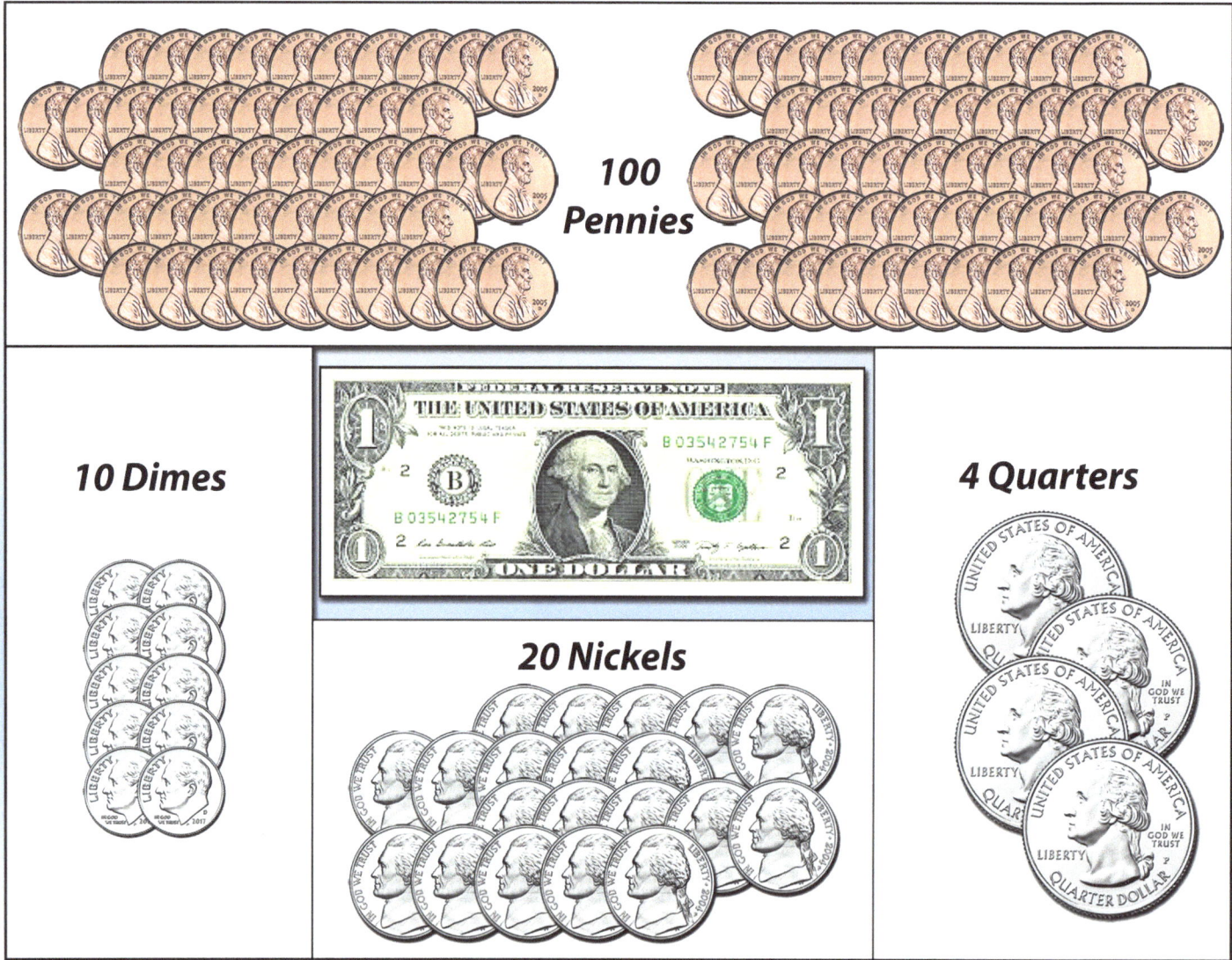

100 Pennies

10 Dimes

20 Nickels

4 Quarters

How many other ways can you make a dollar by adding coins?

Mommy Hess says to Penelope, "Hurry up, it is time to leave for school; you have a big day ahead of you."

"Make sure you respect your teachers," Mommy Hess says. "Be kind to your classmates and if you cannot say something nice, do not say anything at all." "Yes, Mommy Hess, I know, and I'm going to teach the class that coins add up..."

FAMILY RULES
KEEP YOUR WORD
TELL THE TRUTH
ALWAYS BE KIND

Coins
Add Up

"A penny to a dollar, right Daddy?" asked Penelope. Daddy Dollar to Penelope, "You learn quick, baby girl! You are our very own Pee Wee Coin Coach."

DISHONEST MONEY DWINDLES AWAY

BUT WHOEVER GATHERS MONEY LITTLE BY LITTLE MAKES IT GROW

Proverbs 13:11 NIV

27

Penelope "The Pee Wee Coin Coach"
Call to Action/Coin Conversation:

On a separate sheet of paper, answer the questions below or start the conversation with your parent/child.

- What are the coin names and value of each?

- Can you name who is on the face of each coin?

- What does it say on the back of each coin?

- How many ways can you make a dollar by adding coins?

- What are your family rules/principles?

- What is your family motto?

QL Walker, dubbed "Q, the Coin Coach" because of her frugality and ability to get a dollar out of fifteen cents was born to a young family in Harlem. It was her father who first encouraged her love for numbers, math and being cost conscious. Q is a certified Financial Education Instructor with a Master's degree in Securities and a Bachelor's degree in Business Administration with over 20 years in the financial service industry. Because of her passion for personal finance, Q began *QuWalk* a financial ministry to empower families and youth, ages 3 and up. She loves helping others and values relationships. Her joy, dedication and love are best seen in how committed she is to serving her family, friends, and community. If you ask her, she will tell you that her greatest accomplishment is being "Mommy" to fraternal twins.

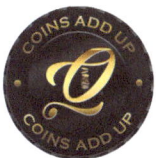

For more information contact Q at qlwalker@coinsaddup.com

Harlem Buck N Up

GROWING
THE FAMILY BUSINESS
Cents Add Up

Penelope's Spending Plan
Serve Save Spend

by
QL Walker

Coming up NEXT..........